Dedication

I would like to thank my leadership students, past and present, who have been my inspiration and given me the motivation to keep on going.

Sometimes it is other people who see us as a champion. It is through their eyes that we have an opportunity to see ourselves as something different from what we know. - *Robin Ray*

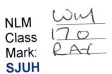

Let's Talk About Stress

A Simple Approach Making Stress Work For Us.

By Robin Ray

Let's Talk About **Stress**

A Simple Approach Making Stress Work For Us

Robin Ray

Published 2017

First Printing: 2017

ISBN:978-1—365-70190-0

Published by Robin Ray

Search for me on Facebook under: Robin Ray Writer

Order more books by contacting the publisher

Special discounts are available on quantity purchases by request. For details please contact the publisher.

Table of Contents

.

Acknowledgements

My whole-hearted acknowledgement goes to my family and friends. I am lucky enough to have these people in my life who inspire me with love and creativity.
I am grateful. Robin

Notes

Robin Ray

After teaching leadership classes in Santa Ana, California for over 15 years I realize that all of us have a great need to deal with the stress we have in everyday life.

Many students have told me that stress management was one of their favorite classes. That is what inspired me to write this book.

Introduction

Stress is described as:

"Anything that stimulates you
And increases your level of alertness"

Some of the physical factors that go with stress are:

- Increased heart rate
- Intensified awareness
- Higher sensitivity
- Tightening of muscles

When we are playing sports, dancing, singing, cooking and cleaning we are under some stress. People often think of stress as only a bad thing. The things that cause stress are often called 'stressors'.

Some good things in life can cause stress too. Can you think of some?

What can happen when there is negatively perceived stress:

- Headaches
- High Blood Pressure
- Upset Stomach
- Road Rage
- Rashes
- Strokes
- Depression
- Anger Problems
- Heart Disease
- Low Self-esteem
- Divorce
- Weight Gain
- Weight Loss
- Insomnia
- And many more

Yikes! I stepped in the mud

We can let stressors of life really rule us if we are not careful. Knowing the long term effects of negative stress can help us decide on the changes we may want to make in our life.

What effects does stress have on you?

_____

_____

_____

_____

_____

Positively perceived stress can result in making life more exciting, fun and meaningful! While some positively perceived stress may cause temporary frustration and irritation, the result can actually enhance your life!

Some positively perceived stressors are:

- A new job
- Education
- Love
- Marriage
- Family
- Friends
- Exercise
- Children
- Achieving success
- Personal growth

Can you think of more positive stressors?

_____
_____
_____
_____

When does a positive stressor become a negative stressor?
The answer is: "When you think it does".

Every person is different in their levels of stress. How we think about things (this is called perception) which leads us to a positive or negative perception of something. Some people even enjoy having more stress than others. For example: an extreme athlete encounters many stressful situations.

When we are happy, we are not burdened by stress.
To find out where we are the happiest, we should become more aware of how we feel and think about things. Only then can we determine how happy we are.

*

It is through mistakes that we can make opportunity!

"I went to take a photo of the dog in the car
And I took a photo of myself by mistake"

Let's look at the stages of sustained (long term) stress and the potential harm it can cause.

Beginning of Negative Stress	*Stress Continues*	*Unrelieved Stress*	
- Tiredness - Discomfort - Irritation - Backaches - Headaches	- Anger - Depression - Unhappiness - Exhaustion - Illness	**Major illness** Psychological problems	**Terminal**

The above symptoms can progress over time. The important thing to remember is that a person's *Quality of Life* is affected.

Many of these symptoms and other symptoms caused by stress can and do cause permanent damage to our body, and that affects our wellbeing.

This is why it is so important to deal with the things in life that causes us stress. Denial and not dealing with what cause you negative stress is never a good idea.

It is always a good idea to face the challenges in life that cause negative stress, otherwise we may be destined to live a life of pain and anger both physically and mentally.

Some Signs of Short Term Stress

- *Performance suffers*
- *Become easily overwhelmed*
- *Minor illness*
- *Insomnia*

The key for anyone to find where he or she is happiest is to pay attention to when you are feeling negatively stressed.

*

What events and what conditions make you feel negatively stressed?

When you are aware of the things that make you feel negatively stressed, then you can change them or think of them in a different way?

Remember some stress is needed to make our lives more interesting

---

Low Stress versus High Stress

Low stress = Low Performance + Low Motivation = Boredom

"I am so bored; there is nothing to do"

High Stress = Low performance + Low motivation = Anxiety

Finding your balanced stress level will give you the best performance!

"Working with a grumpy Extraterrestrial is too stressful!"

8 STEPS

An 8 step process to help you manage your stress

An 8 Step Process to Manage Your Stress

1. Take at least 3 deep breaths when stress is present.

A deep breath is taking a breath from your diaphragm, not your chest. Breathe in from your nose and slowly let your breath out through your mouth. This will slow down your heart rate so you can handle the stressful situation calmly.

2. Become aware of things that cause you stress and how you react to them.

Take notice of the situation(s) that cause you stress. Try not to ignore them! It is best not to deny that a problem exists.

Look at it and notice your reaction to it.

What causes you stress?

_____
_____
_____
_____
_____
_____
_____
_____

Go ahead and write in your book; it will help you process the information.

3. **Recognize what you can and cannot change.** Can you permanently change a stressful situation by avoiding it or eliminating it? Or can you shorten your exposure to things or people that cause you stress?

<u>Some ideas to handle stress</u>

➤ **Taking classes for personal development**
➤ **Talk with someone who may understand your situation**
➤ **Go out and have some fun**
➤ **Visit a nature setting that you find relaxing**
➤ **Listen to music that gives you a peaceful feeling**
➤ **Read or view inspirational books or other media**
➤ **Be proactive in keeping yourself healthy**
➤ _____
➤ _____
➤ _____

List some of your favorite ways to relieve stress in the spaces above.

4. **Determine how you are looking at the situation.**
Our thoughts are very powerful. As a matter of fact, how we think about something determines how we react to it.

Can you think of something from a new point of view?

5. Learn to moderate your Physical Reactions to stress.

When you know a stressful situation is going to happen, you can prepare yourself ahead of time by using relaxation techniques such as deep breathing techniques, prayer and/or meditation.

If a stressful situation happens without warning, can you take a minute to compose yourself before reacting? The key here is to keep your heart rate down and lesson the tension in your muscles.

When you have learned to control your physical reactions to stressful situations then you have more control of what happens next!

*

What is something you can do to relax yourself if you know a situation is going to be stressful?

_____

_____

_____

_____

6. Build up your Physical Reserves.

It is important to maintain good health. Poor health can be stressful and cause stress in others. When you have the ability to take care of yourself, it is in your best interest to do so. Some kind of stress is guaranteed to happen at some point; by keeping yourself in premium health, you give yourself an extra boost against fighting stress.

Some tips to maintaining good health:

- **Set aside personal time so you can recharge**
- **Participate in something you like to do consistently**
- **Practice looking at the positive side of things**
- **Lessen the use of alcohol and smoking**
- **Eliminate unnecessary drug use**
- **Get regular exercise**
- **Make healthy food choices as often as you can**
- **Spend time with people you like to be around**

What is a new healthy habit you can create to increase your Physical Reserves?

_____

_____

_____

7. **Maintain Emotional Provisions.** It is meaningful to have supportive relationships, people you can count on to support you through rough times (and people who can count on you in tough times as well).

Tips on gaining and maintaining emotional provisions:

- **Develop good communication skills to preserve and develop good relationships.**

- **Lesson your exposure to people who don't have your best interest in mind.**

- **Don't let disappointment paralyze your happiness.**

- **Give consideration to people in your life that have your best interest at heart.**

- **Change is imminent. Be flexible enough to roll with changes as they occur.**

- **Set personal boundaries for yourself in order to have personal peace.**

- **Seek spiritual or religious support if that is what you feel would be of personal support.**

- **Offer emotional support to people but don't take on their problems as your own to solve. Personal growth happens when people learn to solve their own problems.**

   Who is someone you can count on to help you through stressful events in your life?

   _____
   _____

   What is one thing you can do to improve and maintain your emotional provisions?

   _____

8. Be Kind to yourself. What you think of yourself often reflects in how you treat other people.

- **Create and nurture really good relationships**
- **Look for positive outcomes in stressful situations**
- **Learn to become a problem solver**
- **Associate with optimistic people**
- **Decrease the negativity in your life**
- **Forgive yourself if you make a mistake**
- **Forgive others if they make a mistake**

What is one thought you have of yourself that you like?

_____

_____

_____

What is one thought you have of yourself that you don't like?

_____

_____

_____

Is there anything you can do to change what you do not like about yourself?

_____

_____

_____

_____

_____

_____

* This book is meant to be a reference guide. As with any information you receive, when you first read it, take what appeals to you in the moment. *Feel free to make personal notes in the book.* I hope you will find something valuable each time you read this book.

Turning negative stress into something valuable is possible...

...Robin Ray

Notes

Notes_____

_____
_____
_____
_____
_____
_____
_____
_____
_____
_____
_____
_____
_____
_____
_____
_____
_____
_____
_____
_____
_____
_____
_____
_____
_____
_____
_____
_____
_____
_____
_____
_____

Date your notes so you can see how you progress

The Prospective Sign

Poem by Robin Ray

See life as an adventure to take
Risk often for adventures to make
Look back … Not in regret
But
Look forward to things you haven't done yet!

Hume Lake , California

Tehachapi, California

We would all like to live here on the corner of
Easy Street andWhy Worry Lane! – ☺ Robin Ray

References

All content in this book are all creations made by Robin Ray.

This includes text, poems and photos (exceptions were noted).

*Robin Ray's personal photos provided by:

Wyman Gentry Photography

For further information contact: wymangentry.com

Notes:

Notes:

CPSIA information can be obtained
at www.ICGtesting.com
Printed in the USA
LVHW04s1829240518
578383LV00002B/322/P